A MARRIAGE MINUET

David Wiltse

BROADWAY PLAY PUBLISHING INC
56 E 81st St., NY NY 10028-0202
212 772-8334 fax: 212 772-8358
BroadwayPlayPubl.com

First printing: June 2007
I S B N: 0-88145-342-0

Book design: Marie Donovan
Word processing: Microsoft Word
Typographic controls: Ventura Publisher
Typeface: Palatino
Printed and bound in the U S A

ABOUT THE PLAYWRIGHT

David Wiltse is the author of eleven plays and twelve novels. He is the recipient of the Drama Desk Award for "Most Promising Playwright", and the Edgar Allen Poe Award.

Mr Wiltse is currently the Playwright-in-Residence at the Westport Country Playhouse in Westport, Connecticut.

The world premiere of A MARRIAGE MINUET was
produced by Florida Stage (Louis Tyrrell, Producing
Director; Nancy Barnett, Managing Director), opening
on 21 October 2005.

REX	Stephen Schnetzer
DOUGLAS	David Mann
LILY	Laura Flanagan
VIOLET	Kate Levy
GIRL	Autumn Horne
Director	Wendy Goldberg
Scenic design	Kent Goetz
Costume design	Anne Kennedy
Lighting design	Suzanne M Jones
Sound design	Matt Briganti Kelly
Choreographer	Karma Camp

CHARACTERS & SETTING

DOUGLAS, *a literature professor, naive, noble, thirty-five to sixty*

LILY, *his wife, bright, sophisticated, thirty-five to fifty-five*

REX, *best selling novelist, happy philanderer, fifty-five to sixty*

VIOLET, *his long suffering wife, thirty-five to fifty-five*

GIRL, *twentyish, sexy, plays many parts*

Setting: The environs, homes, and shops of an East Coast college town

Time: The present

ACT ONE

*(The set is free form. Since the play is not realistic
in presentation, the set need not be representational.
If modules or furniture are to be used, they should be
designed so that the actors can simply push them from
one area to another as they continue acting. The emphasis
throughout should be on simplicity.)*

*(A note on style: Action should be continuous and scene
breaks are only conceptual and should not involve curtains
or lights. When actors address the audience and then the
characters, the transition should be rapid, a mere twist of
the head. A line of dialogue denoted "to us" means that it
is a thought and it may or may not be addressed directly to
the audience. Generic dialogue, such as "barely suppressed
irritation" or "false sympathy..." should be delivered directly
to the other actor as if it were real dialogue. The emphasis
in the sex scenes should be on the dialogue, not on physcial
presentation. At no time should the physical aspects be
graphic or specific. The GIRL will play several roles and she
can wear something simple to denote a different character,
such as a wig or an apron, but no attempt should be made
to actually disguise her.)*

*(Ideally the graphics should be on a Vaudeville style card but
if more convenient, they can be projected, drop on placards,
or any other way as long as the actors can appear to change
them themselves by hand or gesture. The graphic itself should
have the capitalized words on the top line and the indicated
scene, a store, the bedroom, etc., on the second line. If a choice*

*must be made because of space or other consideration, use the
"graphic" and drop the "scene".)*

(At rise: A burst of eighteenth century music. DOUGLAS
and LILY, REX *and* VIOLET *dance on in a highly stylized
four-handed dance of the period that we are calling a gavotte.
[It may or may not actually be one.])*

(Graphic: THE DANCE)

(Scene: Where you will.)

(The foursome are involved in the dance when the GIRL *walks
past.)*

(Enter GIRL. *She crosses, passing the dancers.* REX *sees her,
disengages from the others and dances/run/pants after the*
GIRL. *They both exit.* DOUGLAS *lingers as the other dancers
dance off.* DOUGLAS *observes* REX's *panting pursuit of the*
GIRL *and then changes the graphic.)*

(Graphic: HIGHER EDUCATION)

(Scene: A junior college classroom.)

*(*DOUGLAS *stands behind a lectern.)*

DOUGLAS: Well, now, I'm glad you asked that question,
Mister Cohn-Bertolli, even though you thought you
were being facetious, even though you hoped you were
giving your coed chums a hoot and a giggle and an
illicit, cheeky twit at the stuffy professor. The difference
between the literature of the nineteenth and early
twentieth centuries and the self-involved, solipsistic
acts of public onanism that pass for the novels of the
man you refer to as your "favorite writer" ...and
favorite is a word better applied to flavors of ice cream
than a single selection from among the thousands of
authors worthy of admiration—is that Dickens and
Austen and Dreiser considered it their duty to instruct
the reader in the oft delayed, tortuously arrived at but
always edifyingly uplifting effects of living a moral life.

They did not glorify brain-eating, heroin-abusing, sociopathic behavior as elements in a well-rounded, ethically instructive, rich, full existence. It is the presence of morality that imparts meaning and lifts literature, and life, from the merely trivial.
(He changes the graphic. Continuing; to us, of Cohn-Bertolli)
Back-stabbing favor-currying weaseling little tweedle...
(He changes graphic, exits.)

(Graphic: THE QUEST ETERNAL)

(Scene: A book store)

(The GIRL *is taking inventory of the shelves.* REX *enters. He walks past* GIRL, *ostensibly checking the shelves for something but actually eyeing her speculatively. He passes her once, does a loop, returns and eyes her again.)*

REX: *(To* GIRL*)* Excuse me...Excuse me.

GIRL: Yeah?

REX: Dictionary of synonyms?

GIRL: Aisle three.

REX: I looked there, I couldn't find it. I wonder if you'd be good enough to show me.

*(*GIRL *sighs in annoyance.)*

GIRL: Barely suppressed irritation.

REX: *(Smiling)* False sympathy for the under paid and under appreciated.

*(*GIRL *leads him elsewhere. [A large circle ending at same bookshelf will do.] He eyes her appreciatively as they go.)*

REX: *(Continuing; to us)* I infatuate so easily. It's a curse. My heart is a hostage to beauty.

REX: *(Continuing; to* GIRL*)* Ingratiating chit-chat.

GIRL: Total lack of interest.

REX: *(To us)* When the light catches the plane of the cheekbone at just the right angle. A turn of the neck. A smile of any kind, shy, incandescent, polite, embarrassed...

(GIRL *offers cheekbone, turn of the neck, smile, all just before he mentions them and without seemingly paying any attention to him.)*

(GIRL *reaches for the product on the shelf.)*

REX: *(Continuing; to us)* A flexing of the calf muscle... that tender spot behind the knee...so vulnerable.

GIRL: It should be right here.

REX: *(To us)* I hid it...A face on a billboard, anything. I mooned for months over a drawing of a woman on a can of pinto beans.

GIRL: I'll look in the back. *(She exits.)*

REX: I'll look forward to your return. *(To us)* Once infatuated it drives me insane, because what if that's really *her*? What if that's the woman who will delight my days and enchant my nights and do things to my life that will be transcendent and profound... Never sure what exactly...I have such pangs of loss that I don't have her—until I can discover something, anything wrong with her. If I find a woman in all things perfect yet her hips are too wide does it not follow that somewhere out there is a woman in all things perfect whose hips are just precisely wide enough to effect my fulfillment? Virtually any flaw will do.

(GIRL *enters, carrying book.)*

GIRL: Is this what you wanted?

(REX *pretends to look for glasses.)*

REX: I forgot my reading glasses. Could you tell me what this word is?

(REX *opens the book at random and points to a word while holding book down and far enough away that the* GIRL *is forced to bend over to read it.* REX *studies her at close range while pretending to read the page.*)

REX: *(Continuing; to us)* No warts, shell-like ears... I'm lost.

GIRL: *(Citing the word)* "Annoyance—nuisance, pest, bother."

REX: I'm glad they keep the old favorites. Thank you so much, it's so good of you to help me. You're as efficient as you are beautiful. *(He smiles.)*

GIRL: *(To* REX*)* Pretending pleasure at the compliment while ignoring the implications. *(She gives him a big, phony smile. Continuing, to us; of* REX*)* Too old, too smarmy, too obvious. *(She exits.)*

REX: *(To us)* She shows too much gum when she smiles. What a relief. *(He shrugs, dismissing her, and puts the book back on the shelf. He changes graphic and exits.)*

(Graphic: DOMESTIC BLISS)

(Scene: Chez Zweig)

*(*DOUGLAS *is still steaming about Cohn-Bertolli.)*

DOUGLAS: *(To himself)* Back-stabbing favor-currying weaseling little tweedle... Insolent, zit-pocked, pustulant, teen-aged literary poseur... *(To us)* Snarling, he enters his cave.

(A blast of contemporary music.)

DOUGLAS: *(Continuing; yelling off)* Turn it down, Howard...Howard! ...Howard!!

(The music abates.)

DOUGLAS: *(Continuing)* I said turn it down... Because it's loud and moronic, that's why...Bach, that's who's so hot...Bach does not sound like a metronome! *(To us)*

Sacrilegious ungrateful little whelp...Snarling, he enters his cave. *(To himself)* Notes for the novel. Chapter three. Snarling, he entered his office... *(Seeking the* mot juste) ...to go to work...to start work...to begin work...to work... Like a modern day Grendel, his office littered with the bones of dismembered students, the man snarled and set to work...commenced working...began to labor... *(To us)* This is the writer in his cave, the slow sifter of words agonizing over a vacuum, inspiring life onto a blank page and quickening the dead ciphers of the alphabet with the febrile breath of imagination. Like a sorcerer incanting charms, like an alchemist with his vials and alembics...

(Enter LILY.*)*

LILY: Douglas?

DOUGLAS: I'm working.

LILY: Were you talking to yourself again?

DOUGLAS: It's called musing.

LILY: How do I look?

DOUGLAS: Beautiful, as always.

LILY: Do you think I've gained weight?

DOUGLAS: *(To us)* Trick question. Only one answer.

LILY: *(To us)* Taking much too long.

DOUGLAS: No.

LILY: Maybe I need to do more sit-ups.

DOUGLAS: You do sit ups?

LILY: Every night, you know that. And leg lifts.

DOUGLAS: I've never noticed.

LILY: What did you think I've been doing flat on my back with my legs in the air?

DOUGLAS: I assumed it was a spiritual practice.
Didn't want to pry.

LILY: You're in your hateful mood, aren't you?
What happened today?

DOUGLAS: Cohn-Bertolli, the snotty little hyphenate.

LILY: I thought you told me he was smart.

DOUGLAS: Smart as iodine on an open wound.

LILY: *(To us)* Whatever happened to iodine?

DOUGLAS: But no respect for his betters. He took
it upon himself to point out that Hemingway is a
posturing bore—it's my job to point that out, not his,
and I take an entire, deferential semester to do it.
Now this adenoidal lout ruins my lesson plan in three
sentences. His idea of literary criticism is thumbs down
and a rude noise, like a movie review... Is it too late to
take a job with you in real estate?

LILY: You're too honest for that, sweetheart.

DOUGLAS: Why do I do this, can you tell me? Why do
I spend my days trying to teach literature to a bunch of,
oh, let's just call them "students", shall we, and then
come home and try to write novels? What ails me?
I am yoked to literature like Prometheus to his rock.
A harmless youthful enthusiasm for Kipling doggerel
and adventure stories, lost boys kidnapped by Indians,
Gunga Din saving the day—somehow transmogrified
into a lifetime defending Virginia Woolf.

LILY: *(To us)* I love it when he speaks in paragraphs.
(To DOUGLAS*)* You know you love it.

DOUGLAS: As a leper loves his bell.

LILY: Don't forget the Franklins are coming over tonight!

DOUGLAS: The Franklins! Why not roast me on a
skewer? Why are we entertaining the Franklins?

LILY: We owe them.

DOUGLAS: We can't stand them!

LILY: That has nothing to do with it. We have to repay them.

DOUGLAS: If we repay them, they'll think they owe us.

LILY: You like Rex.

DOUGLAS: I don't like Rex. I thought you liked him.

LILY: Why would I like him?

DOUGLAS: Do you mean the Franklins have wormed their way into our affections under false pretenses?

LILY: At least you have something in common, you're both literary men.

DOUGLAS: Rex Franklin is not a literary man. He is a concocter of best sellers, a boiler of pots.

LILY: His last book was number one on *The New York Times* list.

DOUGLAS: Despite a rather prolonged downturn the American public is not yet such an ass as to make a Rex Franklin assemblage number one on the best-seller list...it was only number seven. You have to make a decision. Do you want your work to be something you're proud of, or do you want your paperbacks displayed at the check-out counter of every supermarket, convenience store and pharmacy in this whole illiterate nation?

LILY: I don't think it would hurt an author's reputation as a serious novelist if his book sold a little...I don't mean you, personally.

DOUGLAS: My latest book did sell a little. *(To us)* Damn little. She's having her revenge for the weight exchange. *(To her)* It just never found its audience.

LILY: Who was its audience and where were they hiding?

DOUGLAS: I like to think Henry James would have enjoyed it.

LILY: Does he buy many books?

DOUGLAS: *(To us)* Flushed though we are with regular sluicings of marital joy there is always a little acid remaining in the creases. I don't hold it against her. I know I'm not easy.

LILY: Artistic injustice aside for the moment, the fact is we get along fine with the Franklins even though you don't like them, and we all need friends, imperfect though they may be.

DOUGLAS: Are we back to the Franklins? I thought I was holding forth on art and literature.

LILY: You were through. At least you agree that Violet is a lovely woman.

DOUGLAS: Lovely? Meaning some feminine spiritual affinity incomprehensible to men—or actually good-looking?

LILY: Don't you think she's attractive?

DOUGLAS: I don't think I've noticed.

LILY: Oh, Douglas, we've known them for six years. Are you going to tell me you don't think she has gorgeous eyes?

DOUGLAS: Does she? What color are they?

LILY: Where do you live? How can you write and be so unobservant?

DOUGLAS: I see what interests me. What are they, blue, brown?

LILY: You're narrowing the field.

DOUGLAS: I haven't paid any attention. She's never said more than three words in a row to me.

LILY: We've had the longest talks!

DOUGLAS: Only when you and Rex are in the room. If we're alone she gets this frightened, mousy look and stares at the floor and mutters something about her children. I don't want to terrorize her further so I mumble something about Howard and then we sit in silence until you come back.

LILY: Maybe you intimidate her.

DOUGLAS: Me? Why?

LILY: Sometimes you act so—you know—intelligent.

DOUGLAS: Good God, do I? How embarrassing for you.

LILY: I know you don't mean it. She likes you.

DOUGLAS: What makes you think that?

LILY: A woman can always tell.

DOUGLAS: Then why doesn't she talk to me?

LILY: Maybe because you always choose a topic. People don't want to discuss anything, they just want to talk. You can be so dense, sometimes.

(She kisses him, chastely. He puts a hand on her hip. They freeze for a moment in this semi-embrace.)

DOUGLAS: *(To us)* Sex?

LILY: *(To us)* Sex?

(They hold the pose, contemplating the possibility, then break apart.)

DOUGLAS: *(Covering)* I had to tell Howard about his music again.

LILY: You certainly know when he's in the house.

(LILY walks away from him.)

DOUGLAS: *(To us)* ...She wasn't fooled.

LILY: *(To us)* It's been so long. Even a casual touch is an embarrassment. Actual sex would seem—impolite... I have to lose weight. *(She exits.)*

DOUGLAS: *(To us)* What has happened to my libido? I love her, she is my support, my comfort, my happiness, my solace, my wife. I adore every line and wrinkle in her face and I'm responsible for most of them. My lady wife. I have no greater treasure...why don't I want to sleep with her? *(He changes the graphic. He exits.)*

(Graphic: FRIENDS)

(Scene: The same)

(Enter REX, his wife VIOLET, and LILY.)

REX: Wonderful meal, Lily. General expressions of satiety. Heaps of fulsome praise for the feast.

LILY: Demurrers, pretense of modesty.

REX: Egregious encomiums for under-cooked fish and over-cooked string beans.

LILY: *(To us)* It seemed to go over rather well. *(To him)* I'm so glad you liked it.

REX: Lily, you are as masterful in the kitchen as you are beautiful in the...bath. Bathroom. *(To us)* Christ!

LILY: Pardon me?

VIOLET: *(To us)* Jerk.

REX: ...as you are lovely in the living room. Pretty in the parlor. Stunning on the street.

LILY: Does he go on like this all the time, Violet?

VIOLET: *(Sourly)* All the time. *(To us)* But not to me... If he talks about himself any more tonight, I may scream.

(Enter DOUGLAS.)

DOUGLAS: So, Rex, working on anything new?

REX: Well, I have the seven book contract, you know. Very lucrative, of course, but a real ball and chain. Still four more to go but the last one did so well we're going to renegotiate.

VIOLET: *(To us; screaming)* Arrrrhhhhhhhhhh!!

REX: It's currently number three in *The Times*.

(DOUGLAS holds up seven fingers and mouths "Seven!")

LILY: Is the next one going to be about Nazis, too?

DOUGLAS: You write about them so often one suspects a secret fondness for the Third Reich.

REX: Oh, those naughty Nazis. But you got to love the uniforms. And what other group can you malign with impunity these days?...Of course I like to think the popularity of my books is due to the fact that I write about real people. Relationships, isn't that what life is really all about?

VIOLET: *(To us; like a dog)* Howwwwuuuuuhhh!

REX: But there's a secret to a really popular book beyond that. Do you know what it is?

DOUGLAS: Very close similarity to ever other really popular book?

REX: It's the first sentence. You've got the have a really great first sentence.

DOUGLAS: "It was the best of times, it was the worst of times..."

REX: Yeah, what's the rest of that?

DOUGLAS: I don't remember.

REX: That's my point. Now try this. "Sergeant Heinrich of the Waffen S S cocked his Luger and stuck it in the suspect's mouth." Now that's a great first sentence, if I do say so myself. Grabs you by the gonads, doesn't it?

LILY: That's how I experienced it.

REX: Do you know what makes that sentence work?

VIOLET: *(barks)* Arf, arf, arf!

REX: It's the word "Waffen". It's attention to the significant detail, that's what writing is all about.

DOUGLAS: Do you happen to know a literary critic named Cohn-Bertolli?

REX: Now your last book...what was it called?

DOUGLAS: "Scapegrace."

REX: *(To us)* What the hell is that?

VIOLET: *(To us)* A rogue or scoundrel. I had to look it up.

REX: Catchy.

DOUGLAS: I wanted to title it *Stephen King's Latest Hit* but the publisher wouldn't let me.

REX: How did it do? Pretty well?

DOUGLAS: *(To us)* Like all my books, it was published as a secret document. *(To him)* Oh, you know...

LILY: It sold very well. We were very pleased.

DOUGLAS: *(To us)* I love her.

REX: Delighted to hear it.

DOUGLAS: It sold well into the three figures.

REX: *(Laughs)* Ha ha ha! *(To us)* Including remainders. *(To them)* What's the new one about?

DOUGLAS: The difficulty of living a moral life in a society without real values or morals.

REX: Your books are always about that. You're kind of a scold, aren't you, Dougie? Although I must say I admire your...

LILY: Who would like an after dinner drink?

DOUGLAS: *(To us)* For pity's sake, don't keep them here any longer!

REX: Splendid idea. I'll help you.

DOUGLAS: *(To us)* And don't leave me alone with her!

(LILY exits, followed by REX. DOUGLAS and VIOLET are left alone. They look at each other very quickly. VIOLET immediately looks at the floor.)

DOUGLAS: *(Continuing; to us)* I'd sooner have a weight attached to my scrotum. *(To VIOLET)* So, how are the kids?

VIOLET: *(To us)* He always wants to talk about our children. Being a good father is a very appealing quality in a man. *(To DOUGLAS)* I loved your last book.

DOUGLAS: *(Pause; to us)* Hark! *(To her)* Really? I didn't know you'd even read it.

VIOLET: I've read all your books. Several times. I love them. I think you're the best unrecognized serious novelist in the country.

DOUGLAS: *(To us)* Except for the "unrecognized" bit...

VIOLET: You treat morality as if it is a vital part of our lives, you're not afraid of big ideas, your style is both lambent and explosive...

DOUGLAS: *(To us)* More more! ...Just to clarify. *(To her)* I'm very glad you think so.

VIOLET: Your characters are real human beings with elaborate thought processes and complicated but honest emotional responses.... No wonder you don't sell well.

DOUGLAS: *(To us)* Right now I'll forgive her anything.

VIOLET: I think you're great.

DOUGLAS: *(To us)* Her eyes are blue. *(To her)* Thank you, Violet. How nice.

VIOLET: I mean it. I think you're absolutely wonderful.

DOUGLAS: *(To us)* This woman is underrated.

VIOLET: *(To us)* He has always been very kind to me. The older you get the more you appreciate kindness.

(LILY and REX enter. LILY changes the graphic.)

(Graphic: THE "LONNNGGG GOODBYE")

(Scene: The same)

(All four are trying with little success to hide expressions of boredom.)

VIOLET: *(Continuing)* Lily, that was such a delicious desert.

REX: *(Agreeing)* Oh!

DOUGLAS: Um!

VIOLET: You must give me the recipe. *(To us)* She makes it every time.

(Pause, pause, pause. No one has anything to say.)

REX: Encroaching deer population...Lyme disease... Nile virus...Plague.

LILY: Expressions of concerned agreement.

DOUGLAS: Ditto.

VIOLET: *(To us)* If I hold my breath long enough he will have a heart attack and die. Starting now.

(VIOLET holds her breath. Pause, pause, pause.)

LILY: Our President is a half wit.

REX: You're too generous by a quarter.

DOUGLAS: *(To us; despairingly)* They've eaten a free meal, it's nine o'clock, why won't they go?

(Pause, pause, pause)

LILY: *(To us)* I overcooked the green beans.

REX: *(To us)* I think I could have Lily. I think she's available.

DOUGLAS: *(To us)* Chapter three. Baring his teeth in a Waffen snarl, the writer entered his blood soaked cave...

(VIOLET is struggling with her breath holding.)

LILY: *(To us)* Tedium.

REX: *(To us)* Boredom.

DOUGLAS: *(To us)* They'll never leave!

(VIOLET is all but clawing the furniture in an effort to hold onto her breath.)

LILY: Violet, are you all right?

VIOLET: *(gasping)* Fine.

REX: She does that quite a bit these days. Just stops talking for the longest time. People will think you're crazy, Violet.

DOUGLAS: She seems to me a woman of very sound judgment, actually.

VIOLET: *(To us)* If I do five hundred Kegel exercises, starting now.

(N B: VIOLET's Kegel exercises should actually lift her off her seat in a way that the audience can see it.)

LILY: Concern over college admissions.

REX: Sympathy.

VIOLET: *(While Kegeling)* Encouragement.

LILY: Discouragement about S A T scores.

VIOLET: Sympathy.

REX: Encouragement.

LILY: But he's really very smart.

VIOLET: *(Still Kegeling)* Supportive tales of other friends' stupid children.

DOUGLAS: *(To us)* Upon entering his cave, the snarling writer put the Luger in his own mouth...

REX: My, look at the time.

(No one looks at the time, but all quickly agree.)

DOUGLAS: As late as that?!

LILY: The time just flew.

REX: Have to get up in the morning because of some lame excuse.

LILY: Gratitude and understanding.

DOUGLAS: Sympathy, encouragement.

VIOLET: *(To us)* Fifty seven, fifty eight...

(All rise. REX and VIOLET approach the exit, turn to say goodbye, and all four suddenly gush and fawn with an enthusiasm they haven't shown all night. Tedium and discomfort are swept away with relief that the evening is over and replaced by immense conviviality that is almost sincere. They speak simultaneously in a headlong burst.)

VIOLET:	LILY:
It was so nice of you to have us over. It has been too long, we must do this again soon, you have to give me that recipe, I mean it, and I just love what you've done with the living	We're so glad you could come, it's been too long, we must do it again soon, oh, it's very simple really, just cream and eggs and sugar and gelatin and, exercise sounds wonderful

room, let's get together,   I've gained some weight I
we could go to exercise   know it...
class....

REX: *(Simultaneously; to* DOUGLAS*)* So this guy and this
girl go horseback riding and they come to the woods
and get off the horses and they're lying on a blanket...
(His voice rises over the others.) ...and the male horse
mounts the female horse and starts going at it,
ka-thoom, ka-thoom, ka-thoom...

(The women stop and regard REX *who is demonstrating a
piston motion to go along with the sound effects.)*

VIOLET: *(To us)* I should kick him.

REX: ...and the guy looks at the girl and says "now
that's what I want to do." And the girl says, "go ahead,
it's your horse."

DOUGLAS: Embarrassed laughter

LILY: Ditto.

REX: Joy unconfined!

*(*VIOLET *draws one foot back as if to administer a kick.)*

REX: *(Continuing)* You're standing funny, Violet.
What's that about?

*(*VIOLET *adjusts her stance so it seems to be something
other than preparation for a kick.)*

VIOLET: Cramp.

REX: So, listen, let's get together again real soon.

ALL: Yes, oh yes, yes, yes, yes, yes, *yes!*

*(*REX *and* DOUGLAS *shake hands, the women embrace.
Then* VIOLET *embraces* DOUGLAS*, shyly.* REX *engulfs*
LILY *in a hug.)*

REX: I can't let go. What is this? Her attraction is too
powerful. Release me, Lily, release me.

VIOLET: Let her go, Rex. You're embarrassing everyone.

REX: It's no use, I'm stuck on her.

VIOLET: *(To* DOUGLAS*)* Get the hose. *(To* LILY*)* Don't worry, Lily, it never lasts.

REX: Guess you'll just have to let me keep her, Dougie.

*(*REX *walks around, holding onto* LILY *as if they're stuck.)*

VIOLET: *(Sternly)* Rex!

*(*VIOLET *gives his ear a violent twist.)*

REX: Ow! What's that about?

(But he releases LILY*.* VIOLET *exits.)*

REX: *(Continuing; to* DOUGLAS*)* All in jest. *(To* LILY, *confidentially)* Wink, wink. *(He changes the graphic and finally exits.)*

(Graphic: THE POSTMORTEM)

(Scene: The bedroom)

DOUGLAS: A night without end!

LILY: I think we're the only normal couple we know. Is that possible?

DOUGLAS: If by normal you mean one in a thousand, you're absolutely right.

LILY: We are lucky, aren't we?

DOUGLAS: *(To us)* This sense of us against our friends may be the best part of marriage...safely cocooned in our mutual embrace we lie just a comfortable inch or two the wrong side of smug. You can build a great wall without mortar, the Incas did, but how securely conspiracy serves as cement. *(To her)* What was going on with you and Rex?

LILY: He was only flirting.

DOUGLAS: I wonder why he hasn't been shot.

LILY: Because you can't take him seriously. He's like a boisterous St. Bernard puppy. That's not the kind of flirting to worry about.

DOUGLAS: Short of looting and pillage, what else could he do?

LILY: It's not what you do, it's the attitude. A woman can tell when a man is flirting seriously just by the look in his eye.

DOUGLAS: I can't.

LILY: You are so naive about that kind of thing. You're probably being flirted with all the time and don't even notice.

DOUGLAS: I wouldn't know what to look for.

LILY: I know, bless your heart. It's nothing to worry about, it's just a little game some people play to make themselves feel attractive.

DOUGLAS: I don't like the idea of someone playing games with my wife for any reason.

LILY: Oh, don't be so disapproving. You just don't understand it because you're never tempted to do it but you get no credit for that, it's like praising a eunuch for chastity.

DOUGLAS: *(To us)* Neutered for a simile.

LILY: Flirtation is just a harmless little gavotte, done in seconds with a smile and an innuendo. No one is hurt by it. No one expects to be taken too seriously. Look, level one. Serious eye contact. *(She looks at him intensely. Continuing)* Level two. *(She touches his arm. Continuing)* Note the touch..."Oh, could you help me lick this stamp? I can never seem to do it right." ...Still retractable if he doesn't respond...Level three. "Oh, you have an eyelash." *(She touches his face to remove the eyelash. Continuing)* Of course if he doesn't respond to level one and two, you don't go to level three. Both of you have to be playing the game.

DOUGLAS: Level four?

LILY: I don't know, I've never gone past three.

DOUGLAS: So, how do men flirt?

LILY: Men get awkward, do something stupid, show off. They're not real subtle.

DOUGLAS: Anything else?

LILY: They put aside their self-absorption for a moment and actually pay attention to you.

DOUGLAS: That's it?

LILY: It comes as a shock to know we're being listened to. We notice. But if they really want to get to us, they make us laugh.

DOUGLAS: Ka-thoom, ka-thoom. Go ahead, it's your horse.

LILY: He just makes himself laugh.... Flirting is mostly meaningless. But I'm glad you care.... Do you really think someone could still be attracted to me?

DOUGLAS: I'm still attracted to you.

LILY: I mean a man.

DOUGLAS: Husband as castrato.

LILY: You know what I mean.

DOUGLAS: You mean could another man look at the external package of natural beauty and cosmetic enhancement, the flawless features, the taut skin, the still sagless parts, could he inhale the heady mix of floral essence and musk of civet cat with which you mask your own, more beguiling odors, could he hear the gentle bell-like tones of your tinkling laughter, watch the glitter of your teeth, the flash of your almond eyes, could he take in all of this and still not be attracted to you? Is that what you mean?

LILY: Precisely.

DOUGLAS: Only if he were made of stone.

LILY: You're a sweet man, Douglas.

DOUGLAS: *(To us)* I may know nothing about the *gavotte* of flirtation, but I do understand the cakewalk of marriage. Whoever said "honesty is the best policy" must have been a bachelor.

(LILY gives him a kiss of gratitude. They freeze.)

LILY: *(To us)* Sex?

DOUGLAS: *(To us)* Sex?

(They nuzzle a bit.)

LILY: *(To us)* Rex is not without charm in his stag-in-rut sort of way.

DOUGLAS: *(To us)* When Violet said I was absolutely wonderful, did she mean just as a writer?

LILY: *(To us)* Sex?

DOUGLAS: *(To us)* Sex?

BOTH: *(Pause)* Yes.

(They embrace and make love in a stylized way. Like bad sidewalk-mimes in slow motion, they merely suggest touching each other, etc. Alternatively, the actors can remain still and the changes can be indicated by lighting. In either case, specific and graphic gestures should not be used.)

LILY: *(To us)* It's been so long. A little tentative to begin with.

DOUGLAS: *(To us)* One has permission, still, no wish to take undue license.

LILY: *(To us)* Ah. That feels familiar.

DOUGLAS: *(To us)* It comes back to me now. A certain ritualized behavior. A well practiced protocol.

LILY: *(To us)* More like baking than cooking. A specific amount here, a precise amount there.

DOUGLAS: *(To us)* Like opening a safe. Twist a knob, press a button, insert key in lock..."Absolutely wonderful?" What did Violet mean exactly?

LILY: *(To us)* Rex's boisterous puppy dog act has an appeal in its overzealous canine way.

DOUGLAS: *(To us)* Listening for the clicks as the tumblers fall into place.

LILY: *(To us)* Nothing wrong with vanilla.

DOUGLAS: Patience... Do unto others as you would have them do unto you.

LILY: Gone to all this trouble, might as well...

DOUGLAS: *(To us)* And so...

LILY: It's so-oh-oh-oh! eeeeasy when you trust him.

(The miming ends.)

DOUGLAS: *(To us)* Success. Rush of masculine pride. Virility reconfirmed...Felt good, too. *(To LILY)* Exclamations of delight. Mutual congratulations on our carnal excellence. Vow of eternal love. Promise of more frequent sexual relations in the future.

LILY: Ditto.

DOUGLAS: *(To us)* I really mean it... Every time.

LILY: *(To us)* I know he means well.

BOTH: *(To us)* This is love.

DOUGLAS: *(To us)* Or is it just marriage?

(REX enters, changes graphic. DOUGLAS and LILY exit.)

(Graphic: THE RAKE'S PROGRESS)

(Scene: A book store)

(Enter the GIRL, *wearing glasses, book in hand, perusing bookshelves. She is a customer this time, not the employee.* REX *does a reconnoiter, passing her, doing a loop and returning.)*

REX: *(To us)* When I can't find anything wrong with her, it drives me mad with longing. All of me, All of me demands that I have her or lose my last chance for salvation. And yet I require so little disillusionment to calm my heart; gum chewing, nail-biting, fake nails, nose piercing, tattoos, bad breath, bad attitude.

*(*GIRL *reaches above her for a book.)*

REX: *(Continuing)* ...and so little to excite it. A well-muscled bicep and I'm weak in the knees. What do I imagine that bicep ever doing with, to, or for me? I don't know, I can't think of anything, perverse or innocent, and yet, right now, I'd risk anything for it. *(To* GIRL*)* This is a great book.

*(*GIRL *looks at it doubtfully, then recognizes his picture.)*

GIRL: That's your picture!

REX: You have me.

GIRL: Instant, generic attraction to celebrity.

REX: Yes, I know.

GIRL: Coupled with a particular bent towards literary figures, the result of a sickly, bed-ridden childhood. I can't believe it's really you.

REX: In the flesh.

GIRL: What a coincidence!

REX: Imagine.

GIRL: Would you, I mean, could you autograph it for me? *(She removes her glasses.)*

REX: *(To us)* Signs...

GIRL: To Cindi, with an "i". *(She primps with her hair.)*

REX: *(To us)* ...and signifiers.

(He autographs. She reads it, touches his arm.)

GIRL: Oh, that's so sweet.

REX: *(To her)* Pretty, pretty, pretty, pretty, pretty, pretty, pretty. *(To us)* They like that.

GIRL: No, really...

REX: Lovely, fair/beyond compare/full of beauty/ you're a cutie. *(To us)* They can be plain as a post and still believe it. *(To GIRL)* Some flatulent book talk as a reminder of status.

GIRL: Not fooled for a second but willing to make an exception to good judgment given the attraction to fame and power.

REX: Good enough for me.

(Enter DOUGLAS and LILY. They see REX, watch him work his magic. He does not see them. REX exits, his arm around GIRL.)

(DOUGLAS and LILY watch them go.)

LILY: It certainly does look like it.

DOUGLAS: The effrontery of the man!

LILY: Do people still have effrontery?

DOUGLAS: Aren't you shocked?

LILY: Not really.

DOUGLAS: How many mistresses does he need before you get offended?

LILY: I don't need to get offended, darling. You do that for both of us. I love that about you.

DOUGLAS: We should tell Violet.

LILY: Absolutely not.

DOUGLAS: How can you be so blase?

LILY: In the first place, it's none of our business. In the second, she probably wouldn't appreciate it.

DOUGLAS: Wouldn't you want to know?

LILY: Douglas, nobody wants to know. If you don't know, you don't have to do anything, you don't have to make any decisions. This is a time for blissful ignorance. Besides, what makes you think she doesn't know already?

DOUGLAS: She knows he's having an affair?

LILY: Probably. Women usually do.

DOUGLAS: Why does she put up with it?

LILY: He's rich, he's famous, which means she is too, sort of. He doesn't abuse her, he's the father of her children, they have a life she's used to, she's no longer twenty-three, she has obviously developed a high tolerance for Rex if she can put up with him at all— and maybe his affairs take pressure off of her... There are at least as many reasons to put up with him as toss him out.

DOUGLAS: How can she take him into her bed knowing he's been with another woman?

LILY: Oh, they haven't been sleeping together for several years.

DOUGLAS: How do you know that?

LILY: Violet told me. Frankly, I think she's a bit relieved. Rex is apparently not the world's greatest lover.

DOUGLAS: Just the most active.

LILY: And his tastes are not quite as straightforward as you might think.

DOUGLAS: The things one woman will confide to another. A husband stands naked before the world of wives. Do you tell her personal things about me?

LILY: No! *(To us)* Of course. Intimacy is the currency of women's conversation.

DOUGLAS: The idea of discussing your sex life as if it were the President's... What does he do?

LILY: Do I have your interest?

(She starts off, he follows.)

DOUGLAS: Come on, Lily, don't leave me hanging, what does he do?

(DOUGLAS changes the graphic, they exit.)

(Graphic: CONQUEST)

(Scene: The GIRL's bedroom)

(Enter REX and GIRL.)

REX: *(To us)* This one is not my heart's ease. Just an opportunity.

GIRL: My roommate, husband, mother, child won't be home for a long time.

REX: Oh, baby, baby, baby...

(They assume an embrace of sorts. The sex in this sequence is also mimed, but in a less formalized, more improvisational way.)

GIRL: *(To us)* What am I doing?

REX: Oh, baby, baby, baby...

(REX puts his hand over her breast in an exaggerated way, his hand actually at least a foot away from contact.)

GIRL: *(To us)* Why am I doing this?

REX: Oh, baby, baby, baby...

(REX *puts his other hand on her ass, in the same elaborate way.*)

GIRL: *(To us)* What is he doing?

REX: *(To us)* The first time is never any good. They do so many things wrong. *(To* GIRL*)* Oh, baby, baby, baby...

REX: *(Continuing; to us)* Too much tongue there, too much movement there, oh, way too hard there...

GIRL: *(To us)* Ouch, slow down, not there, not that, not now, not that way...

REX: Oh, baby, baby, baby!

GIRL: *(To us)* He needs me so much. It would be churlish to refuse. *(To* REX*)* Oh, you great big man!

REX: *(To us)* I love it when they call out, even if it's not my name. A woman called me Myrtle once, turned out it was her pet iguana. I didn't mind...I was confused, but I didn't mind. Oh, give me a screamer every time.

GIRL: *(To us)* Will this never end? *(To* REX*)* Oh, Mister Franklin!

REX: *(To us)* Okay, doing the multiplication tables now... State Capitals... Counting backwards from a hundred... Sergeant Heinrich of the Waffen S S stuck the Luger in the suspect's mouth... Come on, Secretariat!!

GIRL: Whee!!

His head droops, the embrace ends. She straightens her clothes.

REX: *(To us)* Instant, overwhelming distaste for any further involvement. Flee with leave-your-leg-in-the-trap desperation. *(To* GIRL*)* Wonderful, great, good for you?, got to go, call you soon.

GIRL: *(To us)* Well, what can you expect from a trophy fuck? I can't wait to tell the girls. *(She exits.)*

(Graphic: ELEMENTARY, MY DEAR WATSON)

REX: I regret the choice of woman, but not the accomplishment. Afterwards, alone, I revel in the sheer roguery of it. What a charming rascal I must be, smoking behind the corn crib, fooling the teacher, cheating the I R S. Don Juan is a villain only at the opera. Lonely nights, empty times, cruel reviews— I can comfort myself with the knowledge of how successfully bad I have been. I forget the women but remember the conquest, the score, the number. It's one more on the life list. I philander for the arithmetic.

(REX changes the graphic and VIOLET enters.)

REX: *(Continuing)* Hideeho, and so to house and no one the wiser.

(Scene: Bedroom)

VIOLET: Where have you been today?

REX: Oh, facile lie, barely adequate excuse. *(To us)* No tell-tale matchbook in the pocket, no alien hairs on my jacket. Scrubbed and polished. Home free.

VIOLET: Complacent acceptance of a lame story.

REX: *(To us)* Know your enemy. *(He exits.)*

VIOLET: *(To us)* He's at it again. Lingering smell of foreign soap, hair still damp, wearing his underwear inside out. She is clearly five foot three, left-handed, a 34-B. *(She crosses to graphic, changes it.)*

(Graphic: A LITTLE KNOWLEDGE IS A DANGEROUS THING)

(Scene: Coffee shop)

(VIOLET sits at a table.)

(DOUGLAS *enters.* VIOLET *sees him, he does not see her at first.* VIOLET *studies him for a long time.*)

VIOLET: *(Continuing; to us)* Why not? *(To him)* Doug? Doug?

(DOUGLAS *sees her, crosses to her.*)

DOUGLAS: Well, what a happy coincidence and other general niceties.

VIOLET: Mild expressions of pleasure. Would you like to join me?

DOUGLAS: *(To us)* No. Potential awkwardness, nothing to say, wide-ranging social ineptitude. *(To her)* Well, actually...

VIOLET: I've been thinking about our last conversation.

DOUGLAS: Sure. *(He sits quickly.)*

DOUGLAS: *(Continuing; to us)* Waiting to be admired.

VIOLET: I was just thinking how presumptuous it was of me to tell you about your own books. I'm only a high school teacher.

DOUGLAS: Not at all.

VIOLET: You know how good they are without my telling you, don't you?

(She fixes him with her gaze.)

DOUGLAS: God, no. I have such a list of possibilities in my mind. They're great, they're pretentious, they're awful, they're mediocre. Did you know that "mediocre" comes from the Latin meaning "halfway up the mountain"? I have this vision of mediocre me with a pen in my hand, stuck forever on some precarious ledge halfway up a slope that is hopelessly beyond my ability to climb.

VIOLET: You're a very serious man, aren't you?

DOUGLAS: Yes, I guess I am. Kind of boring, isn't it?

VIOLET: I like it. I can't bear to think that the whole world doesn't tell you all the time how good your work is.

DOUGLAS: The whole world and I are currently not speaking.

VIOLET: *(Laughing too much)* You're so funny!

DOUGLAS: *(To us)* She thinks I'm funny! *(To her)* Go ahead, it's your horse!

VIOLET: *(Laughing harder)* No, really!

(She touches his arm.)

DOUGLAS: *(To us)* Good God! Like an electric shock, straight to the groin!

VIOLET: I really should call Lily and make a date for dinner. It's our turn.

DOUGLAS: *(To us)* Her hand is still there!

VIOLET: You have a little something...

(She reaches for his face. He flinches.)

VIOLET: *(Continuing)* You jumped. Did I frighten you?

DOUGLAS: Did I? No, I didn't.

VIOLET: Just a little eye lash.

(She reaches for his face again to remove something. He leans far back to avoid her, she pursues him and finally manages to do it.)

VIOLET: *(Continuing)* You're not afraid of me, are you?

DOUGLAS: Of course not. *(To us)* Now, as I understand it that was one, two and three...wasn't I supposed to do something? Something a man does? What was it?...

VIOLET: I'll call Lily about getting together.

DOUGLAS: *(gasp)* Lily! *(He exits.)*

VIOLET: *(To us)* Don't I deserve something? Is it
never my turn? Rex is out there like a mink in heat,
marking the trees. It's a wonder he hasn't been shot in
a henhouse by now. I'm a fool to put up with it without
fighting back...Besides, I want Douglas, I want him.
I want to know what he's like, I want to know how he
thinks. I want him to want me. I want him to lie awake
scheming how to be alone with me, how to get up the
courage to touch me. All that noble posturing—I want
it done in my bed. I want the furtive thrills of meeting
on the sly, I want the sweet longings of deprivation.
I want him to desire me with every aching inch of his
body. Aren't I entitled to some attention, some warmth,
someone who thinks I matter? ...And besides it's so
exciting! *(She changes the graphic and exits.)*

(Graphic: THE PLOT THICKENS)

(Scene: Chez Franklin)

(REX enters, very pleased with himself.)

REX: *(To us;)* Heaven help me, I just screwed the maid!
Is there no end to my depravity? What a rogue and
peasant slave am I. Well, I'm not to blame. There's
something about a maid, all that tropical immigrant
sexuality roiling around in an empty house, flapping
the bed linens. *Le droit de Seigneur* and all that, I am a
slave to tradition.

(GIRL enters, as the maid. She curtsies coyly.)

GIRL: Senor.

REX: Senor, Seigneur; what's in a vowel?

GIRL: Green card, you no forget. *(She exits.)*

REX: Green card, absolutely, as promised. *(To us)* Oooh,
what an imp I am. I marvel at myself, led penisforth to

my destiny.... Someone stop me before I turn on the
pets. *(He changes the graphic and exits.)*

*(Graphic: SOME TEDIOUS MORALIZING. IT'S GOOD
FOR YOU.)*

(Scene: College)

(DOUGLAS enters and stands behind the lectern.)

DOUGLAS: Because, Mister Cohn-Bertolli, life is a stern
moral enterprise whether you realize it or not and the
price of folly is destruction. It is all too easy to think of
yourself as the rogue stag, mocking the milling herd,
but the herd will survive, the herd will shape the
history of the species. The herd *is* the species and those
pedestrian, bovine ways that you deride are their
protection. The lone stag will be devoured by the lone
wolf and all his lupine pals. Without the discipline and
anchor of the middle class, the world is like Ghana and
the Balkans and the Ivory Coast. The choice is structure
or chaos and those who espouse destruction of the
framework on which our culture stands are like the
teenager who mocks the work ethic of his parents
but shows up regularly for his three free meals a day.
(He changes the graphic and exits.)

(Graphic: TAKE HEART. ALMOST INTERMISSION.)

(Scene: Chez Franklin)

(Enter REX and DOUGLAS.)

REX: What's wrong, Dougie? Why so glum?

DOUGLAS: This is just the way my face falls when I'm
thinking.

REX: You look like that all the time.

DOUGLAS: Need I say more?

REX: Has your writing got you down? Does it feel like
passing a pumpkin?

DOUGLAS: Elegantly and accurately put.

REX: A little tip. When you're stumped, when you don't know what to write next, throw in a sex scene. That's what I do.

DOUGLAS: I've noticed.

REX: Of course you have to name some of the body parts to do it right. Your sex scenes are a bit abstract. "He pleasured her." Pleasured her? Dougie, ka-thoom, ka-thoom. That's what they want.

DOUGLAS: Everything isn't about sex.

REX: Sure it is. You can't look at an ad for a toilet bowl cleaner without seeing a sexy babe. We've got bimbos and bimbettes and bimbellas dancing and jiggling a conga line through our lives.

DOUGLAS: That is not the essence of a decent life.

REX: Ah, but it is. We live in a universe of sexual signals, they're pulsing through the ether like gamma rays, you can pick them up on the fillings in your teeth.

DOUGLAS: They're not pulsing through my universe. I'm happily married.

REX: Oh, come on. Marriage is the greatest aphrodisiac there is. Two months after I got married I was lusting for every other woman I saw.

DOUGLAS: Not every man has other women on the side.

REX: They have or they want to or they will. Anyone who denies it is as sanctimonious as a U S Senator. Do you think our wives don't have sex on the brain, too? Listen to the conversation tonight and I'll lift my hand every time they really mean sex.

(*Enter* VIOLET *and* LILY, *talking.*)

LILY: So, once you've soaked the beans, you get three pounds of sausage...

VIOLET: That much sausage?

(LILY *indicates a length with her hands.*)

LILY: At least that much. You can't have too much sausage as far as I'm concerned.

(REX *lifts his hand to indicate sex.*)

REX: Well, okay, that's too easy. *(To all)* How about those Mets?

LILY: Oh, men and their bats.

(REX *lifts his hand.*)

VIOLET: What is it with men and balls, anyway?

(REX *lifts his hand.*)

REX: *The New York Times Magazine.*

LILY: Beginning to sag, I think.

(REX *lifts his hand.*)

VIOLET: They're just not up to it anymore.

(REX *lifts his hand.*)

DOUGLAS: How do you think free trade effects the G N P?

(*They stare at* DOUGLAS *in silence.*)

REX: Who wants coffee?

LILY: I'll help.

(REX *and* LILY *exit.*)

VIOLET: How is Howard?

DOUGLAS: Oh, fine. How are your...children?

VIOLET: The girls are fine.

(*Graphic: MEANWHILE*)

(*Scene: The Kitchen*)

(LILY *and* REX *enter to the other side of the stage.*)

REX: Can you get the cups?

LILY: *(To us)* I look good in this outfit. *(She stretches for the cups.)*

(DOUGLAS *and* VIOLET *both study the floor for a moment.*)

VIOLET: Douglas. There's something I have to say to you.

DOUGLAS: *(To us)* More praise would be nice.

VIOLET: I don't know how to put it so I guess I'll just say it. It's been building for so long I think I'll bust if I don't get it out.

DOUGLAS: *(To us)* Burst, not bust.

VIOLET: I think I love you.

(DOUGLAS *is stunned into brain silence for a moment. He stares at us in a stupor.*)

(REX *and* LILY *in kitchen.*)

REX: *(To us)* Oh, the legs, the arms, the breasts.
A woman stretches in front of a man at her peril.

(REX *puts his hand on* LILY's *neck, preparatory to a kiss.*)

LILY: Now, Rex...

REX: I have to.

LILY: *(To us)* Oh, well.

(*They have a real kiss, long and lingering. They remain locked in the kiss for the rest of the act.*)

(*Scene: The living room*)

VIOLET: Do you hate me for saying that?

DOUGLAS: *(To us)* No. *(To her)* No.

VIOLET: I was afraid you'd run from the room or give me a lecture about propriety. But since you haven't...what do you think we should do about it?

DOUGLAS: Uhhhh....

VIOLET: *(To us)* I love the crisp cunning of his mind...

DOUGLAS: I, uhhhhh....

VIOLET: *(To us)* He says what he feels and he means what he says.

DOUGLAS: Uhhhh.

(VIOLET *reaches out and takes* DOUGLAS's *hand in hers. He flinches, nearly jumps, but lets her keep his hand.)*

VIOLET: I know. It's frightening, isn't it?

DOUGLAS: *(To us)* Is this level four?

(Graphic: INTERMISSION. SMOKING IS BAD FOR YOU.)

(Curtain)

END ACT ONE

ACT TWO

(Graphic: THE GAVOTTE)

(Again a strain of eighteenth century music. REX and VIOLET enter, dancing in the elaborate, stylized fashion of that age. The dance is different from the one that opened the play, less formal, more sensual. Enter DOUGLAS and LILY. They stop to watch the dance, curiously. VIOLET and REX make gestures for them to join in. Both DOUGLAS and LILY are tempted. REX breaks loose from VIOLET and does a single in front of LILY, not unlike a bird doing a mating dance.)

VIOLET: Why do men always think they're doing it alone?

(VIOLET beckons demurely to DOUGLAS. REX holds out his hand for LILY, she takes it and joins in the dance which is now for three. DOUGLAS is alarmed that Lily has left him but he is powerless to move as the three of them dance off and change the graphic as they exit.)

(Graphic: FOR THOSE WHO MISSED THE POINT SO FAR)

(Scene: College)

(DOUGLAS enters and stands behind the lectern.)

DOUGLAS: No, Mister Cohn-Bertolli, not everyone does it. Some people pay their taxes, return the extra money when a cashier makes a mistake, deposit their litter in the proper receptacle and some— yes, some—turn off their cell phones when they should. You seem to think these people are fools and dupes and schmucks, that they're missing out on the wise guy, corner cutting, leg-up advantages. Well, yes, that's the point. They miss out, they do without, they struggle to lift the impossible weight of their own expectations...but that's precisely the point. Why did Shakespeare write in sonnet form? Because it's difficult and confining and that constriction released his genius.

It's the deprivation, it's the sacrifice that gives value to the experience... That's actually Elizabeth Barrett Browning whose sonnet you misquote, Mister Cohn-Bertolli, but you have the general idea... *(To us)* Iambic pentameter as an ethical determinant. An interesting notion, to be sure, but who can concentrate when there's sex on the agenda? *(He changes the graphic. He exits.)*

(Graphic: THE WORM)

(Scene: En route)

(REX enters. He glances at the graphic, points to himself in disbelief and disapproval.)

REX: *(To us)* I'm not feeling very good. My stomach has come unmoored and is floating loose, pressing on my heart, and my vision is blurred, I keep seeing a face that isn't there, and yet I've never felt better in my life.

(Scene: Beneath LILY's balcony.)

REX: *(Continuing; to us)* What raw magic then is this? We exchanged a simple kiss. I have kissed some several score, yet never felt like this before. Was there some potion on her lips? Some perfect measure of the hips? I am transformed, I am bewitched, and all my rakish plans now switched to stratagems of true desire for Lily's drip to quench this fire. Senses swirling willy-nilly I'll yet find means to gild this Lily.... Ye gods, poetry. The greatest sin of the besotted.

And yet I swear there was something so perfect about

her kiss, a melding of mouth to mouth, when her lips
touched mine I felt that I was melting on the spot.
I have to Have to *have to* have her... Oh, fuckeroo,
I'm in love.

(LILY *enters*)

REX: *(Continuing)* But soft.

LILY: No, Rex.

REX: Please.

LILY: No, it's very flattering, but no.

REX: Why not?

LILY: *(To us)* Persistence is very appealing.

REX: Pretty, pretty, pretty, pretty.

LILY: Thank you. *(To us)* I am no schoolgirl to be
beguiled by simple praise, however well deserved.

REX: Pretty, pretty, pretty, pretty.

LILY: *(To us)* Of course there's something about
quantity, too. *(To him)* I must go now, Rex.

REX: I'll wait for your return. Heedless of the wind and
weather as long as the question's when, not whether.

LILY: You're being silly. *(To us)* Certainly not what one
expects from Sergeant Heinrich of the Waffen S S...
It's only a harmless little flirtation, good for a cheap
thrill and a giggle. *(To him)* Good night, Rex. *(She exits.)*

REX: *(To us)* That's not the same as "go away".
(He changes graphic and exits.)

(Graphic: DEE-FENSE)

(Scene: The Coffee Shop)

*(DOUGLAS enters, sits. GIRL, as waitress, enters and crosses
to him.)*

GIRL: Order?

DOUGLAS: Coffee.

GIRL: *(To us)* He's hitting on me.

DOUGLAS: *(To us)* She seems a nice young woman.

(GIRL starts to exit. VIOLET enters, crosses to DOUGLAS who does not immediately see her.)

VIOLET: Well, hello.

(She touches his arm. DOUGLAS flinches.)

DOUGLAS: Oh, hello.

VIOLET: I always seem to be startling you. I'm sorry.

DOUGLAS: I have sharply honed reflexes, in case of attack—by a saber toothed tiger, for instance.

VIOLET: I'm in good hands then.

(DOUGLAS puts his hand in air to indicate a sexual innuendo as REX taught him.)

DOUGLAS: Well, this is a pleasant surprise. How are you?

(DOUGLAS offers to shake hands. She ignores it an gives him an air kiss.)

GIRL: Order?

VIOLET: Coffee.

GIRL: *(To us)* Bitch. *(She exits.)*

VIOLET: How are you, and other chit-chat?

DOUGLAS: Stammering, hesitant, confused response.

VIOLET: I hoped I might hear from you.

DOUGLAS: Back and fill, buck and wing.

VIOLET: I know, it's difficult, isn't it? I'm having trouble with it, too. *(To us)* But enjoying every minute. *(To him)* Are you sorry I told you?

DOUGLAS: No. *(To us)* Heaven help me, I'm not. *(To her)* And I'm very flattered, Violet, I really am. Touched and flattered and I don't think I've felt so—scattered—and torn and agitated in my life. And I thank you for that.

VIOLET: It sounds very painful.

DOUGLAS: Well, it is, really, because you see, there's nothing to be done about it.

VIOLET: We don't have to do anything. I'd just like to be with you, and talk. *(To us)* Right.

DOUGLAS: *(Simultaneously; to us)* Right. *(To her)* I mean, well, we're both married, though, aren't we?

VIOLET: I understand. I've embarrassed you, and put you in an awful position. I'm so sorry. The last thing I want is for you to feel uncomfortable around me. I withdraw the remark, all right? Just forget I ever said it and we'll go back to being good friends. And we are good friends, aren't we and other face-saving nonsense?

DOUGLAS: Violet...

VIOLET: I understand, I really do, and I admire you for it. Let's say no more about it, we'll just go on the way we were, no hard feelings. All I want is what's best for you, no matter what.

DOUGLAS: Thank you.

VIOLET: *(To us)* I've cheated on my husband only twice and only once was serious. You can't really count the time with the old boyfriend at the reunion. That was unfinished business. Besides, I'd slept with him before I got married anyway, so I wasn't giving away any secrets...I think that's pretty good.

(VIOLET changes graphic. DOUGLAS and VIOLET exits.)

(Graphic: SEEN IN A DIFFERENT LIGHT)

(Scene: Bookstore)

*(G*IRL *enters. This is the bookstore girl from before. She wears glasses and is looking through the shelves again.* R*EX enters. He does not see* G*IRL at first as he looks for the right shelf.)*

REX: Poetry, poetry... *(To us)* Poetry is a vile thing. Unless the author is certifiably dead, I won't even look at it. And if it doesn't rhyme, what makes it poetry? Still, there are those times... *(Aloud)* Poetry, poe... Good lord!

(He has spied the G*IRL, who does not see him. Rex bends out of sight beneath the shelf.)*

REX: *(Continuing; to us)* A former conquest! What's she doing here? I hate meeting people out of context.

(He peeks over the shelf, ducks down again.)

REX: *(Continuing; to us)* Friends, family, golfing partners...a place for everyone and everyone in her place.

(He peeks again. The G*IRL is safely looking away from him. He studies her for a moment.)*

REX: *(Continuing; to us)* I so seldom see them in full light...I'm used to looking at my women at extremely close range so my vision is blurred which does wonders for the aesthetics— My, I have undiscriminating taste when opportunity arises.

*(G*IRL *exits.* L*ILY enters. She does not see* R*EX.)*

REX: *(Continuing)* But soft.

*(L*ILY *goes directly to the shelf she wants and kneels to tend to the book.)*

LILY: *(To us)* I make a weekly sweep of the local bookstores, tending to his latest novel... Two copies here last week, still two copies here today. Sometimes I'll move one somewhere else so that if he comes in and finds only one he'll think he's actually sold the other. Of course I don't know that he checks, he doesn't admit

to it... Turn it so it's facing outward like they do with
the bestsellers... Sometimes I'll put one on the bestseller
table but someone always moves it back...I really wish
they sold better, it would make him so happy. They're
good books. Hard to read and rather boring, but good...
I wish it didn't feel quite so much like taking care of
someone's grave.

REX: Do you believe in coincidence?

LILY: No, Rex.

REX: I ache, I yearn, I burn.

LILY: No, Rex.

REX: I can't eat, I can't sleep, I'm withering away.

LILY: Ask your wife to help you.

REX: That's cruel.

LILY: She's stuck by you, she's nursed you, she knows
you as no other woman can. What's wrong with her?

REX: She's stuck by me, she's nursed me, she knows me
as no other woman can.

LILY: No, Rex.

REX: You haunt my imagination, I am obsessed by the
thought of you.

LILY: No.

REX: Picture me, but for my bad back, at your feet.
I kiss the hem of your garment.

LILY: Hold still. You have an eyelash. (*She touches his
face, removes the lash, blows it away. Continuing; to us*)
So I give him a little something. It's like petting a dog
that's rooting at your crotch. There's just no way to
ignore him without appearing to enjoy it. (*To him*)
Down, Rex. I'm happily married. (*She exits.*)

REX: *(To us)* The key is perseverance. Keep at them long enough and they'll think they owe you. It's the three date rule writ large... There is no seamless marriage. There are clefts and fissures in the stoutest wall that swell and contract with the matrimonial weather. How small a breach is needed to admit a billet-doux, a whiff of excitement. A seed of desire, wafted by a zephyr of flattery can take root within the crevice and crack the hardest stone... And such practical scheming in no way diminishes the purity of my love. *(He starts to go then returns to the shelf and rearranges things around his book. Continuing; to us)* Just a little housekeeping... Look at those beautiful embossed swastikas on the cover. God bless 'em.

(REX *exits,* VIOLET *enters, Bookstore worker* GIRL *enters.)*

VIOLET: Excuse me. Do you have a book called *The Joys of Adultery?*

GIRL: A knowing look.

VIOLET: For my...mother. *(To us)* I love self-help books although the only people they help are the author and publisher. They're like New Year's resolutions, they make you feel virtuous for upwards of a day.

(DOUGLAS *enters and crosses to the same book shelf, also kneeling.)*

DOUGLAS: *(To us)* Ah, they're displaying it differently. Great! Maybe turned a bit more this way... Book sales are highly alphabet dependent. Look at a shelf in any store and what are the books at eye level? Letters G to N. Grisham, King, Ludlum, McMurtry. Even naughty old Anais Nin. Where do you reach to skim that all important first sentence? Grisham, King, Ludlum, McMurtry. What do you reach out to buy? The same popular villains. How else to explain it? Why rise on your toes to the double "A"s, why bend and stoop? What chance does poor Zweig have, down there in kneeling territory in the far right hand corner? If you have a lumbar condition, you'll never see my books at all. My novels are purchased only by people who have slipped and fallen. I'm very popular with those who are immediately post-seizure. That's why there's never been a best seller from my end of the alphabet since Emile Zola.

(Enter GIRL as the book store customer again. She joins DOUGLAS at the shelf, reaches for a book.)

DOUGLAS: *(Continuing; to us)* Mailer. Pfff!

(GIRL puts the book back, looks lower on the shelf, lower, then lower still while DOUGLAS holds his breath.)

DOUGLAS: *(Continuing; to us)* Be still my heart.

(She selects a book and stands.)

DOUGLAS: *(Continuing; to us)* Zola... Ten years, five novels, and I've never seen anyone reading one of my books, buying one, using it as a door stop. Laboring in obscurity is one thing, but I toil away under the mountain like a troll... And yet, to me, it seems I'm mining gold...but Violet gets them. *(He changes graphic and exits.)*

(Graphic: THE LIE THAT BINDS)

(Scene: Chez Zweig)

(LILY enters.)

LILY: *(On phone)* No, Rex... No, Rex... No, Rex...well, maybe... Oh, I couldn't...I shouldn't... *(Laughs)* You're so funny...we'll see.

(Enter DOUGLAS.)

LILY: *(Continuing; phone)* I have to go. *(She hangs up hurriedly.)*

DOUGLAS: *(To us)* Snarling, the writer entered his cave...notes for the novel... Spring has come. The amorous thinks of his carnal delights, the ambitious plots his career, the talented totes up the less talented who have surpassed him, the untalented who have passed judgment upon him, the unappreciative who ignore him, the unwashed who don't deserve him...

LILY: Hello, darling.

DOUGLAS: Who was on the phone?

LILY: ...Oh, that was just Violet. *(To us)* In the very unlikely event that he checks the caller I D, it's the same number. It's not a practiced deception, I'm just quicker than he is. Most of us are.

DOUGLAS: Violet? What does she want?

LILY: Nothing, just saying hello.

DOUGLAS: I didn't know you two were that close. *(To us)* Was she calling me? Will she let anything slip while talking to Lily? Is there anything to let slip? I've done nothing, my conscience is clear. So why do I feel so screamingly guilty? ...I will arrange a tryst, I mean a meeting, to tell her this must cease. *(He exits.)*

LILY: *(To us)* Well, we're better at it than they are, we just are.

(LILY exits. DOUGLAS enters.)

(Graphic: A HASTY RATIONALIZATION)

DOUGLAS: *(To us)* Believing all I believe, feeling all that I feel, how can I go to her? ...How can I not? I melt inside, I am reduced to gel, I quiver just in contemplation... Do I love her? I don't even know her!

Do I want her? I want something, she's given me the taste for something. Something I didn't know I lacked. I don't even know what to call it. The vocabulary is foreign to me. Intelligence is possible only in a culture in which words have particular, agreed-upon, meanings. All else is point and grunt. *(He exits.)*

(Graphic: ALTOGETHER NOW, "DON'T DO IT!"...UNLESS YOU THINK HE SHOULD.)

(Scene: Chez Franklin)

(VIOLET enters.)

VIOLET: *(To us)* He's coming. My womb is aflutter.

(Enter DOUGLAS.)

VIOLET: *(Continuing)* Hello.

DOUGLAS: Grunt, grunt.

VIOLET: You're so funny.

DOUGLAS: Is Rex here?

VIOLET: He won't be home for a long time.

(Enter REX. He changes the graphic.)

(Graphic: MEANWHILE)

(Scene: LILY's balcony)

(LILY enters. REX sinks to one knee, extends his arms in the suitor's classic pose.)

REX: *(Howls like a wolf)* Howooooh!

LILY: *(To us)* That's so sweet.

(DOUGLAS and VIOLET)

DOUGLAS: Violet...a great deal of beautifully worded noble posturing in which I say this can't go on, we're both too good, too fine, too honorable to sully the institute of marriage and our sacred, atheistic vows...

VIOLET: I understand.

(LILY and REX.)

LILY: *(To us)* You can't tease them forever, it's just not nice. After a certain length of time you have an obligation. *(To REX)* Well...alright. Come on in. But just to talk.

(REX *rises and goes to* LILY.)

REX: *(To us)* Smugly I rise, reconfirmed in my charms—which in no way detracts from my genuine passion for her...well, a little..

(DOUGLAS *and* VIOLET)

DOUGLAS: *(To* VIOLET*)* So, I guess I'd better go. *(He starts off.)*

VIOLET: We could just talk...

DOUGLAS: I don't think...

VIOLET: ...about your book.

(DOUGLAS *turns on his heel, rushes to* VIOLET *and takes her in his arms and kisses her, passionately.)*

REX: I have such pain of longing.

LILY: Well, for mercy's sake.

(REX *and* LILY *embrace.)*

(GRAPHIC: FINALLY!)

(Both couples step behind neck high portable screens such as those used in medical offices, or any other device suitable for hiding. They are concealed behind them except when speaking, and then they show the audience only their heads, at sometimes surprising angles, and the odd limb or two.)

(DOUGLAS *pops up from behind screen.)*

DOUGLAS: *(To us)* My bowels are water. I fear I'm losing control of my sphincter. Not sexy...and yet... *(He vanishes behind screen.)*

(REX *and* LILY*)*

REX: The usual endearments.

LILY: *(To us)* He's awfully good with snaps and clasps and buttons.

(They vanish.)

(DOUGLAS)

DOUGLAS: *(To us; horrified)* I feel graceful as a felled tree sprawled atop this woman.

(He vanishes. VIOLET *pops up.)*

VIOLET: Oh, sweetie, oh lover...

DOUGLAS: *(To us)* Oohhh, don't call me that.

(They vanish.)

(REX *and* LILY)

REX: *(To* LILY*)* Yum yum yum!

LILY: You've done that. I'm ready.

(They vanish.)

(DOUGLAS *and* VIOLET)

VIOLET: *(To* DOUGLAS*)* Oh, Doug, oh, lambie.

DOUGLAS: *(To us)* Or that.

(They vanish.)

(REX *and* LILY.)

REX: Yum yum!

LILY: I'm ready, Rex.

REX: Yum yum?

(They vanish.)

(DOUGLAS *and* VIOLET)

DOUGLAS: *(To us)* I'm awkward, I'm clumsy, I can't seem to find things, where did she put it?

VIOLET: *(To us)* What the hell is he doing?

(They vanish.)

(REX *and* LILY.)

LILY: Come on, Rex.

REX: I can do that. *(To us)* Come on, Secretariat!

(They vanish.)

(DOUGLAS)

DOUGLAS: *(To us)* Who's responsible for this design?
A man needs grips, guideposts, directional signs.
(He vanishes.)

(REX)

REX: *(To us)* Come on, Secretariat! *(He vanishes.)*

(DOUGLAS)

DOUGLAS: *(To us)* Lily always takes care of this part.
(He vanishes.)

(VIOLET)

VIOLET: *(To us)* Where does he think he's going?
...That's not it! *(She vanishes.)*

(REX)

REX: *(To us; worried)* Come on, Secretariat! *(He vanishes.)*

(DOUGLAS *and* VIOLET)

VIOLET: *(To us)* What is the big mystery?

DOUGLAS: *(To us)* Oh, there it is!

(They vanish.)

(REX *and* LILY)

REX: *(To us)* Secretariat? ...I am unhorsed!

LILY: *(To us)* He is unmanned.

REX: *(To us)* A horse, a horse!

LILY: It doesn't matter, Rex. *(To us)* And technically,
it doesn't count, either.

REX: *(To us)* Secretariat?!

(They vanish.)

(DOUGLAS *and* VIOLET)

VIOLET: *(To* DOUGLAS*)* Oh, lover!

DOUGLAS: *(To us)* Who cares? I'm pleasuring her now!
Come onnn, Secretariat!

VIOLET: *(To us; simultaneously)* ...Come onnn, Secretariat!

*(*REX *and* LILY *come out from behind the screen,* LILY
straightens her clothes.)

REX: Never, not ever...

LILY: It really doesn't matter. *(To us)* Just like size and
stamina.

REX: My desire for you was too strong, in a funny way...

LILY: *(To us)* Ho, ho.

REX: I'll do better next time... *(To us)* As if.

LILY: *(To us; simultaneously)* As if.

REX: And other bits of unfounded optimism to cover
my retreat as I slink off... *(He exits.)*

LILY: *(To us)* Never up, never in. *(She exits.)*

(DOUGLAS *and* VIOLET*.)*

*(*DOUGLAS *crosses the finish line, yells in triumph, separates
from* VIOLET *and cries out in despair all in one continuous
move.)*

DOUGLAS: *(To us)* Heeeyaaahhhhwowwwhat have I
done!

*(*DOUGLAS *races off and exits.* VIOLET *straightens herself
and comes out from behind screen.)*

VIOLET: *(To us)* There ought to be a rule. A man can
not reach for his pants while his feet are still in the
stirrups... It's not the orgasm. I can take care of that.
I'd gladly do away with the whole sordid tussle in

exchange for a half hour of gentle touching. Is that so much to ask? *(She changes the graphic.)*

(Graphic: THE AFTERMATH, OR ARITHMETIC)

(Scene: Chez Franklin)

(REX enters, gives VIOLET a big, fake, kiss.)

REX: *(Kissing noise)* Mmmmmwhaaaa!

VIOLET: *(To us)* He's been cheating on me again.

REX: *(To us)* She's totally oblivious. What a wonderful wifely trait.

VIOLET: What were you up to today?

REX: Nothing, really. *(To us)* Which is very close to the truth. *(To her)* How about you?

VIOLET: We got an invitation to a dinner party from the Cohns. She told me the Zweigs were invited, too.

REX: Oh, yes? How nice.

VIOLET: *(To us)* I could never be in the same room with her, she could tell just by looking at me. A woman always knows. *(To him)* Do you want to go then?

REX: Up to you.

VIOLET: I don't think so.

REX: Absolutely not.

(They exit. DOUGLAS and LILY enter. They change the graphic.)

(Graphic: FLAMING GUILT)

(Scene: Chez Zweig)

LILY: Hello, darling.

DOUGLAS: *(To us)* She knows!!

LILY: Anything happen today?

DOUGLAS: *(To us)* I am undone! *(To her)* No. You?

LILY: No. *(To us)* He hasn't a clue. *(To him)* We got an invitation to dinner at the Cohns...Rex and Violet are invited.

DOUGLAS: *(To us)* Oh, god. *(To her)* Do we have to?

LILY: *(To us)* It might be fun to watch Rex squirm. *(To him)* Is there any good reason to say no?

DOUGLAS: *(To us)* I can't talk to her! This is awful! Dissemble to my wife? I don't know how! I tell her everything.

LILY: What's the matter, sweetheart? Aren't you feeling well?

DOUGLAS: *(To us)* There is a canyon of guilt between us, my voice won't carry across it.

LILY: Is anything wrong at school? Are you having trouble with your work? ...You know you'll feel better once you tell me, you always do... Well, whenever you feel like talking to me, I'll be here. *(To us)* Just because I cheated on him— well, almost cheated—doesn't mean I don't love him. *(She exits.)*

DOUGLAS: *(To us)* What have I done! I am wounded! I have injured myself! I have brought silence to my marriage, I have distanced my best and only friend, with my promiscuous spade... *(On the word "spade", he raises his hand to note the sexual undertone. He does it unconsciously. Continuing)* What is the matter with me? Even as I bemoan the wretched loss of intimacy with my wife I revel in some kind of sexual dementia. I am obscurely proud of myself... What have I done? Whom can I tell? The only one in all the world I want to confide in is my Lily. I need comfort, I need advice—things I always got from her. I have no friends to torment with this, she is my friend, she is my counselor, whatever life I live outside my mind I

live with her and through her and for her... Whom can
I turn to?

(Enter REX. *He changes graphic.)*

*(Graphic: A MOST IMPROBABLE CONVERSATION:
FEEL FREE TO TAKE SIDES.)*

(Scene: In confidence)

DOUGLAS: *(Continuing; to* REX*)* So I have this friend
who...uh...met this woman...

REX: *(To us)* Old Dougie Clenched-Bottom has a
mistress. I don't know whether to gloat or lament.
If everyone cheats the rules there are no rules...
so where's my advantage?

DOUGLAS: He can't take it any more. His conscience
is tearing me apart. I will not be parted from my wife
even that much by a dirty little secret. I have to tell her.

REX: Whoa! Never confess.

DOUGLAS: I want my life back, I want my wife back,
I want our intimacy back.

REX: Never confide, never confess. *(To us)* I must find
out who she is. Once they're put into play, they're more
accessible. Fun for one, fun for all.

DOUGLAS: I must tell her.

REX: She doesn't want to know.

DOUGLAS: She must know anyway.

REX: Never assume.

DOUGLAS: I must have guilt written all over—his—face.

REX: Don't flatter yourself. You're not the center of her
attention, she is.

DOUGLAS: I am not made for duplicity.

REX: She is, she's a woman.

DOUGLAS: What I have done is wrong!

REX: All of nature tells us it's not. Even life-long mates cheat, even swans.

DOUGLAS: I am not an animal.

REX: We have to do it. Men are the romantics!

DOUGLAS: It's a sin, it's against the law, it's immoral. I can't live a lie.

REX: Sure you can, you're a man. Suck it up.

DOUGLAS: It's no good, I have to tell her.

REX: She won't thank you for it.

(DOUGLAS exits.)

REX: It's guys like that who give us a bad name. Women never confess. They may get caught, but they never confess. Only men are troubled enough by morality to actually act on it. And yet all of morality is in favor of the women. They got in league with the priests and the sissies and made this stuff up. Lie, cheat, steal, fornicate...those are right up a man's alley. Why would we want to take those things away from ourselves? They encoded hypocrisy and named it Commandment. The women outfoxed us. *(He changes graphic.)*

(Graphic: EPIPHANY, OR HOW TO KEEP A GOOD MAN DOWN)

(Scene: Street)

(Enter GIRL.)

GIRL: Excuse me. Aren't you what's his name?

REX: Yes, I am.

GIRL: Oh, I just loved what-do-you-call-it.

REX: Most kind.

(GIRL touches his arm.)

GIRL: The scene with the girl and the...

REX: Handsome S S Major?

GIRL: Where he...

REX: Was wearing only his iron cross?

GIRL: And she...

REX: Was wearing only his jack boots?

GIRL: That was so...you have a little something on your face.

(She touches his face.)

REX: Thank you.

GIRL: Would you sign my boob? Book?

REX: Happy to. *(He signs and moves on. Continuing; to us)* A very pleasant young woman.

GIRL: I must be getting old.

(GIRL exits. REX stops as the realization hits him.)

REX: *(To us)* Nothing! I felt nothing! First Lily, and now this? Could it be that the old boy's down for the count? Could it be he's stopped bumping against my navel forever? Can I be impotent?
   Oh, please, dear god...let it be true! What a relief! The beast has tugged me around like a cat on a leash since I was twelve years old. Free at last after all these years? No more meaningless trysts, no more humping lampposts, no more panting till I trip on my tongue. Oh, blessed detumescence! At long last I can turn my energies to something meaningful. Charity work, flower arranging. I've always wanted to take a whack at feeding the homeless...I will devote myself to Violet, my true and faithful wife. I have mistreated her, but now I will make all things right...and right after that, world peace.

(REX *changes the graphic but stays on his side of the stage,*
watching DOUGLAS *and* LILY.)

(Graphic: CONFESSION IS GOOD FOR THE SOUL)

(Scene: Chez Zweig)

(Enter LILY *and* DOUGLAS.)

DOUGLAS: Lily, I have something to tell you.

LILY: *(To us)* Uh-oh.

DOUGLAS: I have done something...

LILY: *(To us)* I don't want to hear this.

REX: Don't do it!

DOUGLAS: I have to tell you, I feel so bad.

LILY: *(To us)* So now you want to inflict it on me?
Keep it to yourself.

DOUGLAS: My conscience is killing me.

LILY: *(To us)* Fight it, fight back. You can defeat your
conscience! *(To him)* What is it, darling?

DOUGLAS: Oh, Lily, abject confession of the awful truth.
Appropriate sniveling and promise of reform.

(REX *changes the graphic.)*

(Graphic: THE INEVITABLE QUESTION)

(Scene: The same)

LILY: What does she have that I don't have?

REX: Nothing! *(To us)* Really, nothing. That's what they
never understand. It isn't about them, it's about us.
They've done nothing wrong, there's nothing they can
improve. Weight loss and nose jobs and implants have
nothing to do with it. There is no prevention, there
is no protection, there is no remedy, there is no cure.
And there is no fault, no blame. Your husband didn't
stray because you were inattentive or overweight or

even because he didn't love you. He did it for the novelty, he did it because of the opportunity, he did it for the numbers. *(He changes the graphic.)*

(Graphic: MATTERS TAKE A SERIOUS TURN)

(Scene: The same)

DOUGLAS: Can you ever forgive me?

LILY: No.

DOUGLAS: What?

LILY: No. I won't forgive you.

DOUGLAS: I'll make it up to you.

LILY: You can't.

DOUGLAS: Lily, it didn't mean anything...

LILY: Ah, but Douglas, it did. With you, it did. With someone else, with someone like Rex, it would be meaningless, but not with you. It was too important to you. *(To us)* I see no inconsistency here. *(To him)* You think too much to act idly. Your principles are too important to you to throw them aside for a meaningless act.

DOUGLAS: It was one time, one time.

LILY: All the worse.

DOUGLAS: If I were promiscuous, it would have been all right?

LILY: What's one more hamburger to a fat man? But to a vegan... *(To us)* Oh, Rex, Rex, so what? I never preached fidelity. The only principle I had to overcome was a mild aversion to Rex himself.

DOUGLAS: I can't believe this.

LILY: It doesn't matter if a C student cheats. But the honor student?

REX: *(To us)* I told him. None so blind as he who will not listen.

(Graphic: THE OTHER INEVITABLE QUESTION)

(Scene: The same)

LILY: Who is she?

DOUGLAS: Does it matter?

REX: *(To us)* No.

LILY: Of course.

DOUGLAS: Violet Franklin.

REX: Violet!?

(REX exits to find VIOLET.)

LILY: *(To us)* I am no prude, I am no moralist. I get lost and confused in his maze of ethics, but... *(To him)* You have embarrassed me in front of my friends, you have flaunted it in my face...

DOUGLAS: Lily, I didn't choose this!

LILY: Of course you chose it. No adult is seduced. At most, they are simply encouraged... You must go, Douglas.

DOUGLAS: You don't mean it!

LILY: *(To us)* Well, I do at the moment, with full awareness that I won't later on.

DOUGLAS: Lily, please, you mean the world to me.

LILY: You should have thought of that earlier. Go. *(To us)* My pride is hurt. On a business trip, some one night stand with a slut in a bar...but a married woman? Someone my age? It's insulting.

(DOUGLAS slinks off and exits.)

LILY: *(Continuing; to us)* I will make him pay. I may even put him through the sham of marriage counseling

which seems to be little more than school for divorce.
Anything less and he'll think it's approval... Then I shall
magnanimously take him back. *(She exits.)*

*(VIOLET enters and hurriedly crosses the stage, REX enters in
pursuit.)*

REX: Violet! Violet! *(To us)* Who knew my wife was so
interesting?

(VIOLET, in the cat bird seat at last, turns and beams at us.)

(REX and VIOLET exit. REX changes graphic.)

(Graphic: LAST TEDIOUS MORALIZING LECTURE)

(Scene: College)

(DOUGLAS enters and stands behind the lectern.)

DOUGLAS: Why, yes, Mister Cohn-Bertolli, there is a
certain element of hypocrisy in the moral posturings of
the authors in question, and quick of you to notice, too.
But then what of it? Hypocrisy has a prime societal
value. It keeps us adhering to values we don't really
believe in but think our peers do. With racism in our
hearts we descry those with racism on their lips. With
lust in our loins we condemn those who get caught.
This sanctimony keeps us from running through the
streets like a pack of ravening hyenas...And did you
know that both male and female hyena have the same
external genitalia? I leave it to you to decipher the
significance of that... Some of you may know that this
will be my last lecture in this class. Due to certain
family problems I will be leaving the college and
moving to the city. *(He changes the graphic. He exits.)*

*(Graphic: IT IS BETTER TO BEND THAN TO
BREAK—NUDGE THE HUSBAND. IT'S ALMOST
OVER)*

(Scene: Bookstore)

DOUGLAS: I'll never forget her. She is Woman to me, all I wanted, all I will ever want... My book is facing outward.

(GIRL *enters. She stands next to* DOUGLAS, *perusing the shelf.*)

DOUGLAS: *(To us)* I think of my beloved Lily when I wake, I think of her when I work, I think of her when I go to bed. *(To* GIRL*)* Have you tried this one? *(He stoops to get to the "Z"s.)*

GIRL: I've read Zola.

DOUGLAS: This is Zweig. *(To us)* A large part of me is gone without her, I can not function as a full human being.

GIRL: *(Of the book)* This is you!

DOUGLAS: Alas. *(To us)* I will spend my life mourning her loss. I will spend my life struggling to win her back.

GIRL: *(To us)* He looks so sad and artistic.

(LILY *enters.* DOUGLAS *does not see her.*)

LILY: *(To us)* I've changed my mind... When he left I took stock. Howard is at the age when he needs a father—or a jailer... My thighs now rub together when I walk. I can't wear corduroy for the noise...

DOUGLAS: *(To us)* I'll never get over her. Never, ever. There will never be another...

GIRL: I've always wanted to write. You must be very smart.

DOUGLAS: *(To us)* I've learned an invaluable lesson...what was it again?

GIRL: Where do you get your ideas?

LILY: *(To us)* She's young enough to be my— slightly younger sister.

DOUGLAS: Oh, just from life.

GIRL: That's so funny!

(She touches his arm.)

DOUGLAS: *(To us)* On the other hand, Lily never really appreciated my talent.

LILY: Douglas! Doug!

(He does not hear her.)

GIRL: You have an eyelash.

DOUGLAS: *(To us)* When the light catches her like that...I've always wondered what it would be like with a gymnast, swimmer, ballerina, lumberjack. Ess. Lumberjackess.

GIRL: I want to write sooo badly.

LILY: And that's how you'll write, too. Doug! I forgive you!

DOUGLAS: *(To us)* Oh, if I can just capture that intensity of youth. It will release me, transform me...

(GIRL smiles at him, then starts off. She goes halfway to the exit, looks back at him, smiles beckoningly.)

DOUGLAS: *(Continuing; to us)* Well, after all, it's been a whole month.

(DOUGLAS follows the GIRL.)

LILY: Doug! Douglas!

(He does not hear her. GIRL exits, DOUGLAS follows and exits. LILY is left alone on stage as the reality of being finally alone sinks in on her.)

(Music, the same eighteenth century refrain that began ACT TWO.)

(REX and VIOLET dance on, doing the elaborate step. After a moment, DOUGLAS dances on with the GIRL. He does a bit of

free lance twirling and heel-clicking, the others clap politely.
LILY *reaches out for Douglas but the dancers don't recognize her presence.)*

(Suddenly DOUGLAS *comes up lame from a pulled muscle due to his exuberance. The other dancers continue.* GIRL *looks at* DOUGLAS *with disdain as he tries to keep up. The four of them whirl and swirl around* LILY *then dance off with* DOUGLAS *falling behind and limping badly.)*

(Lights fade, leaving a Spot on LILY, *alone in the dark as the others dance off.)*

LILY: *(Continuing; to us)* Even though he doesn't deserve it, I can't help worrying about him. He's so clueless... To hell with him! Who needs a husband? I will join a book club instead... No, I'll go back to work... No, I'll travel and meet interesting men...no, I'll never have anything to do with another man...no, I'll get a dog...

*(*DOUGLAS *limps back on, no longer dancing.)*

DOUGLAS: *(To us; of* GIRL*)* She doesn't remember Kennedy's assassination—she wasn't even born! She thinks Nixon is an actress! ...I thought clubbing had to do with cavemen...Lily never minded my snoring. God, how I miss her. *(To* LILY, *on one knee)* Abject whining and whinging. Admission of grievous error. Attempt to place blame on evolutionary biology, insufficient breast feeding, the devil... Protestation of endless fealty.

LILY: *(To us)* I've been sleeping so soundly without his snoring.

DOUGLAS: *(To us)* I can't find my keys. How do I iron a shirt? I have no clean socks...all our friends are hers... *(To* LILY*)* I love you.

LILY: *(To us, shrugs)* They're so hard to train, it takes years to break one in. *(To* DOUGLAS*)* You have hurt me very deeply. *(To us)* And scared the hell out of me. *(To*

DOUGLAS) I will distrust you for years until you're old enough that I don't care.

DOUGLAS: That sounds like a good basis to build on. *(He embraces her. Continuing)* I love you, Lily.

LILY: Come on home, Douglas. I'll make up your bed in the guest room.

(They start off together.)

DOUGLAS: Forever and ever and ever...

(Music is heard. GIRL dances on, doing a single to the familiar refrain. She eyes DOUGLAS who can't help looking back at her as DOUGLAS, LILY exit. GIRL keeps dancing and is joined by REX and VIOLET, and then by DOUGLAS and LILY as they enter again. All of them dance together as lights dim.)

(LILY changes the graphic.)

(Graphic: THE END: ALL RISE. THUNDEROUS APPLAUSE.)

(The actors take their bows doing a little dance for five.)

(Curtain)

END OF PLAY